HEALING
THROUGH
PRAYERS

DR. D. K. OLUKOYA

HEALING THROUGH PRAYER

Dr. D.K Olukoya

HEALING THROUGH PRAYERS
© 2011 DR. D. K. OLUKOYA
ISBN 978-978-8424-35-2
Copyright January 2011

Published by:
The Battle Cry Christian Ministries

322, Herbert Macaulay Street, Sabo, Yaba
P. O. Box 12272, Ikeja, Lagos.
www.battlecryng.com
email: sales@battlecryng.com
Phone: 0803-304-4239, 01-8044415

I salute my wonderful wife, Pastor Shade, for her invaluable support in the ministry.

I appreciate her unquantifiable support in the book ministry as the cover designer, art editor and art advisor.

All the Scriptures are from the King James Version

There are more hospitals, more clinics, more and better medical equipments, more and better techniques, both in developed and under-developed countries, yet there are more sick people. I never believed that a day would come in developed countries, when the hospital beds would be so full, patients would be arranged on the corridor, and the doctors would not be able to diagnose the problems of majority of the people.

In the past, there was a school of thought that only people from countries that are over-crowded and poor, or where they are very superstitious, suffer from diseases and sicknesses. Now, things have changed. Even comfortable people who are very rich, have their own diseases, such as heart disease, overweight, cancer, etc.

DIFFERENT STROKES!

One of our pastors abroad told me that one day, somebody who was a pilot called him on his phone and said, "Hello sir, are you the pastor of MFM? "Yes," the pastor answered. He said, "Anything you know how to say, begin to say it now because I have a gun and I'm about to blow my brain out." God helped the pastor, and he was able to convince him not to kill himself. This is another kind of sickness. It is not a Nigerian one; not many Nigerians would want to shoot their brain out.

Sickness and disease are traceable to a number of factors. A number of ailments are rooted in demonic machinations. Doctors find it difficult to either diagnose or cure such ailments. These ailments have simply broken the laws of health.

CAUSES OF HEALTH PROBLEMS
These include:

1. Wrong diet.
2. Lack of rest.
3. Exposure to epidemics.
4. Food poisoning.
5. Addiction.
6. Wrong medication.
7. Unhygienic conditions.

8.   Contaminated food.
9.   Lack of balanced diet.
10. Exposure to carrier insects.
11. Foodless food.
12. Consumption of junk food.
13. Sleeping in rooms without ventilation.
14. Smoke emissions.
15. Expired drugs and canned food.
16. Taking sweet things.
17. Failure to manage allergies.
18. Abuse of the body.
19. Sleeplessness.
20. Eating in dirty restaurants.
21. Obesity.
22. Lack of recreation.
23. Consumption of caffeine.
24. Eating frozen food.
25. Drinking bad water.
26. Failure to eat when not fasting.
27. Exposure to human carriers of germs.

Interestingly, most people do not know the value of good health until they say "prevention is better than cure". It is better to maintain good health, than running from pillar to post only when the state of your health becomes appaulling.

> *"Why should ye be stricken any more? ye will revolt more and more: the whole head is sick, and the whole heart faint. From the sole of the foot even unto the head there is no soundness in it; but wounds, and bruises, and putrefying sores: they have not been closed, neither bound up, neither mollified with ointment."*
> Isaiah 1:5-6

For many today, the scripture above is apt. There is no soundness at all. Most people are sick. Only a few are healthy. A lot of people suffer in several areas of human health and well being; examples are:

1. Dental diseases.
2. Eye diseases.
3. Hearing impairment.
4. Stomach ailments.
5. Stroke.
6. Hypertension.
7. Liver diseases.
8. Internal heat.
9. Paralysis.
10. Respiratory ailments.
11. Renal failure.
12. Cardiac arrest.
13. Pneumonia.
14. Mental, or brain ailments.
15. Arthritis.
16. Old age diseases.
17. Ear, nose and throat sickness.
18. Pile.
19. Sexually transmitted diseases.
20. Asthma.
21. Skin diseases.
22. Menstrual disorder.

23. Speech impairments.
24. Scalp disorders.
25. Bumps and abnormal growth.
26. Lameness.
27. Internal growth.
28. Congenital problems.
29. Skin pigmentation problems.

HEALING AND HEALTH.

"Surely he hath borne our griefs, and carried our sorrows: yet we did esteem him stricken, smitten of God, and afflicted. But he was wounded for our transgressions, he was bruised for our iniquities: the chastisement of our pealce was upon him; and with his stripes we are healed." Isaiah 53:4-5

We are healed? This is an eternal statement. The above passage is in the past tense because it is a settled case. God wants to touch and heal you physically, emotionally, psychologically, mentally, financially, and in every area of life where you are hurting. This is His will.

HEALTH IS COSTLY.

You cannot appreciate the importance of good health until you are sick! Many years ago, a certain man was celebrating his 60ᵃ birthday. People brought cakes, wonderful cards and so many other things as gifts. He was a multi-millionaire but was on a wheel chair. After sometime, the people gathered round him and started to sing a song to wish him a happy birthday. Then one of the guests said to him, "Sir, make a birthday wish." The man said, "What good is it to be rich, if I am forever going to be on this wheel chair. I want to get out of this wheel chair." There are sicknesses. The sickness of the rich is often characterised by complexity.

8

Money cannot buy you health. It may buy you drugs, but cannot buy the medicine from above which God gives free of charge. Unfortunately, there are more sick people in the world today than ever before in history. At a time when there are more doctors, more medication and more hospitals, yet more people are sick.

The only way out is through God's word, which is filled with healing from cover to cover.

> *"And said, If thou wilt diligently hearken to the voice of the LORD thy God, and wilt do that which is right in his sight, and wilt give ear to his commandments, and keep all his statutes, I will put none of these diseases upon thee, which I have brought upon the Egyptians: for I am the LORD that healeth thee."*
> Exodus 15:26

This was a life-saving guarantee to the Israelites. This promise was so effective that so many years later, David could say,

> *"He brought them forth also with silver and gold: and there was not one feeble person among their tribes."*
> Psalm 105:37

None of them was sick.

HEALING POWER
Prophet Isaiah declares:

> *"Is not this the fast that I have chosen? to loose the bands of wickedness, to undo the heavy burdens, to let the oppressed go free, and that ye break every yoke?*
> Verse 8 says, "Then shall thy light break forth as the morning, and thine*

*health shall spring forth speedily:
and thy righteousness shall go before
thee; the glory of the LORD shall be
thy rereward.*"   Isaiah 58:6 and 8

There is living healing power in the word of God. The
Bible says,

*"My son, attend to my words; incline
thine ear unto my sayings. Let them
not depart from thine eyes; keep them
in the midst of thine heart. For they
are life unto those that find them, and
health to all their flesh."*
Proverbs 4:20-22

Another version of the Bible says, "**...And medicine
to all their flesh,**" You find this spread out through
scriptures. That was in the Old Testament. Now, we
have a better covenant.

ALL KINDS OF HEALING
In fact, one out of every seven verses in the gospel is about healing. Jesus Himself devoted two-thirds of His time ministering to the sick (all kinds of sicknesses), ranging from spiritual leprosy (which is a sin), to physical sicknesses. Look at the powerful scripture,

"How God anointed Jesus of Nazareth with the Holy Ghost and with power: who went about doing good, and healing all that were oppressed of the devil; for God was with him." Acts 10:38

"When the even was come, they brought unto him many that were possessed with devils: and he cast out the spirits with his word, and healed all that were sick: That it might be fulfilled which was spoken by Esaias the prophet, saying, himself took our infirmities, and bare our sicknesses." Matthew 8:16

"And Jesus went about all the cities and villages, teaching in their synagogues, and preaching the gospel of the kingdom, and healing every sickness and every disease among the people". Matthew 9:35

"But when Jesus knew it, he withdrew himself from thence: and great multitudes followed him, and he healed them all." Matthew 12:15

So far, we have settled the fact that it is God's will to heal. The next thing is the issue of faith. It is so easy to talk theory, but it is the practicality of it that matters. In Mark 9:18, a certain man was complaining to Jesus about his son. He said,

"And wheresoever he taketh him, he teareth him: and he foameth, and gnasheth with his teeth, and pineth

> *away: and I spake to thy disciples*
> *that they should cast him out; and*
> *they could not."* Mark 9:18

That was his complaint to Jesus. In verse 23, Jesus gave him an answer.

> *"Jesus said unto him, If thou canst*
> *believe, all things are possible to him*
> *that believeth. And straightway the*
> *father of the child cried out, and said*
> *with tears, Lord, I believe; help thou*
> *mine unbelief."* Mark 9:23-24

What he was saying was this, "If my faith has been battered by problems, and has become low, help me." This passage exposes the faith problem which trouble many Christians. Actually, the problem is not the presence or absence of faith, rather it is a struggle between positive faith and negative faith; between belief and unbelief.

14

The truth is that everybody has faith, the difference is how the faith is used. If you do not have faith, you will not buy a tin of milk from the market without asking them to open it. You believe that when you take it home, you will see milk inside, so you have faith. The fact that you sit down on a seat, without checking whether you will fall down or not, means that you have faith. So faith is like the gear in your vehicle which can be shifted forward or backward. It depends on where you are shifting your own. When you shift it forward, you are exercising positive faith, and when you shift it backward, it does not go anywhere.

What does this mean? It means on Monday, you have powerful faith. By Tuesday, the faith is gone. By Wednesday, you have a large one again, and by Thursday, it is gone. Friday, you have it, Saturday, it is gone. Sunday, you have it; forward and backward. Such a person will not go anywhere. This is why the Bible says that a doubter is like the waves of the sea, tossed here and there. It then made a very fearful pronouncement. **"Let not such a man think that he can receive anything from the Lord"**. You do not have to draw up more faith, or try and pump it up until it is very big in size.

FAITH FOR HEALING

Faith simply means, believing what God has said in His word and that He will do what He has said. It is having the confidence that God will keep His promises. Whereas, negative faith has many forms:

1. **Fear:** Fear is a forerunner of calamity, the creator of bad things. It brings captivity, confusion, frustration, inner conflict, tension and defeat. It is the favourite weapon of the enemy. It is negative faith. You have faith, no problem, but you are exercising it in the reverse direction.

2. **Doubt:** Another form of negative faith is doubt. This is cruel and destructive. When there is trouble, a doubter blames God. When there are blessings, a doubter will fear whether it would last. As you are reading this bulletin, you have sufficient faith to heal you of any sickness. It depends on whether you are going forward or backward, or whether it is negative faith or positive faith. The Bible says that "faith without

works is dead". Meaning that, you must act on the word
of God and do what God asks you to do. Faith must be
expressed in action.

You do what God tells you to do and then, expect Him
to do His own side. It was Noah that built the ark, but it
was God that flooded the earth. It was Moses that
stretched out the rod, but it was God that parted the
waters. It was Joshua and his people that marched
around Jericho, but it was God that fell the wall. It was
Elijah that smote the water, but it was God that parted
the water. It was Elisha that threw the stick into the
water; it was God that made the iron's head to swim. It
was Naaman that dipped himself into the water seven
times, but it was God that healed his leprosy. As you do
your own part, He will do His own part. Do not come
to a meeting expecting nothing to happen. Come with
expectancy, believing that what God has said in His
word, you would receive.

17

FEELING FAITH

Many people confuse feeling with faith. Feeling has nothing to do with faith. Our healing is not dependent on how we feel, but what God has promised, and what His word says. There may be no immediate sign of healing when you pray to be healed, but as soon as you are exposed to the healing power of Jesus, your healing has come. When you begin to say, "God has healed me, and by His stripes I am healed", His healing power would be released. It is now your turn to set your faith loose. Activate your faith, so that you can touch the hem of His garment. You may ask, "how can I activate my faith, to be able to drink the medicine from above?" I will tell you.

THE HEALING BOOK

Know that the Bible says, God has given to every man a measure of faith. The fact that you have picked up this book shows that one way or the other, you believe that there is power in the Lord Jesus Christ. This is sufficient to get you through, but if you expect something

18

dramatic to happen before something supernatural happens to you, then you will be hindered.

Beloved, the Bible is a healing book. It teaches, without doubt, that God wants to heal you. Whenever healing prayers are being said, do not take anything for granted because in so many lives, the seed of infirmity has already been planted. It may not have grown to a level where you can recognise it, but if you kill it at the seed stage, it will not develop into anything. Although a serpent is very dangerous, a small boy can destroy it at the egg stage, but once it becomes a big python, it becomes a problem. So, healing prayers are both preventive and curative.

The Bible is a healing book. It depends on whether you believe the Bible, or not. God has said in His word that He would heal you. Do you believe His word? If you believe God, then you have to co-operate with Him for your recovery. This is why some people say, "God said it, I believe it, and I receive it."

19

If Jesus tarries in coming, all of us would have to die one way or the other. It is very sad sometimes when you see some people doing bad things that would shorten their lives, and some others fail to warn them against it. Instead of repenting, they would say, "Please leave me alone, one would surely die of something." If somebody has to die of something, must you speed up the death? Remember that life does not belong to you.

As a believer, even if it is time for you to die, you are supposed to depart in peace, because His servant must depart in peace. I do not believe that a child of God has to be rolling on the floor, crying in pain, or going all over the place and suffering before he dies. If you die out of persecution for Jesus, fine. His servant must depart in peace, if he has to depart at that time. You do not have to be terribly sick before you die.

The best way to die, is for you to close your eyes here, and open them in heaven. Disease is not necessary for death. A righteous person can lie down to sleep, and wake up in heaven. This is why the Bible says,

"Thou hidest thy face, they are troubled: thou takest away their breath, they die, and return to their dust." Psalm 104:29

26
HEALING
KEYS

In this chapter, we shall consider the keys to your healing.

HOW TO BE HEALED

1. **See yourself the way God sees you.** You should say like Apostle Paul: "I can do all things through Christ, which strengthens me". This is how God sees you. You may be looking at yourself somehow. Paul could see what God see's. God does not see you being hospitalized, He does not see you roaming about with infirmities and diseases. He sees you as a person who can do all things, so you need to see yourself the way God sees you. God can see a person one way, and the person could picture himself another way. One of

the outstanding statements of God was to Saul, when He said, "Though you are small in your own eyes, but I have exalted you to be the king of Israel. I made you king and blessed you." See yourself the way God sees you.

2.   Replace every fear with love and power.

2 Timothy 1:7

"For God hath not given us the spirit of fear; but of power, and of love, and of a sound mind."

3.   **Take your burdens to the Lord and leave them there.** Take those burdens to the Lord today and leave them there. Believe that He alone can handle it.

4.   **Confess your healing with your own mouth.** You, speak it with your own mouth. Confess what the Lord has done in your life with your own mouth. Say it to anybody who cares to listen. This is how we can light up our faith.

5.   **Be obedient.** There is something called the obedience of faith. When God says, "Do this," just do it, do not rationalise or analyse His word. Do not even think about the history of the problem, because if you do, you will reduce the effectiveness of the power of God in your life.

*"The Spirit of the Lord is upon me, because he hath anointed me to preach the gospel to the poor; he hath sent me to heal the brokenhearted, to preach deliverance to the captives, and recovering of sight to the blind, to set at liberty them that are bruised, To preach the acceptable year of the Lord."*Luke 4:18-19

It is exciting when a blind person sees, but know for sure that there are different kinds of blindness. There is no blindness as bad as spiritual blindness. Try to take your burdens to the Lord today and leave them there.

24

No matter the hard blows you have received, His power sets at liberty them that are bruised.

The first thing to sort out is spiritual sickness. If you do not do this, the physical healing will not come. Therefore, if as you are reading this message you are not born again, that is you have not given your life to Jesus, it is time you do so. You have to do so, as a first step towards enjoying God's divine blessings.

PRAYER POINTS

1. O Lord, let your hand of miracle, healing and deliverance be stretched out upon my life, in the name of Jesus.
2. O Lord, terminate the life of any sickness in my life, in the name of Jesus.
3. I rebuke every refuge of sickness in my life, in the name of Jesus.
4. Every knee of infirmity, bow, in the name of Jesus.
5. Every spirit hindering my healing, fall down and die, in the name of Jesus.
6. Any power that does not want to see me around, you shall not be seen again, in the name of Jesus.
7. I command death upon all sickness, in the name of Jesus
8. Every power constructing coffin for me, enter into your coffin, in the name of Jesus.
9. Every Jericho of infirmity, fall down and die, in the name of Jesus.
10. I receive my divine healing today, in the name of Jesus.

TOTAL
HEALING

Our topic is carried out from the book of Job. *"But ye are forgers of lies, ye are all physicians of no value".* Job 13:4

We have to cry like this to the Lord because in the Bible, although Jesus never refused anyone who came to Him, yet He did not proclaim healing or universal liberty to all captives. The truth therefore is that, some captives may die in their captivity even though they have encountered the Liberator. Some sick people may die in their sicknesses, despite they have encountered the Healer.

Jesus never proclaimed resurrection for all the dead. For example, the Bible says that when He was at the pool of Bethsaida, there was a multitude of impotent folks; the blind, the deaf, the withered, etc, but he passed by them, picked only one man out, and healed him. When Jesus was at the grave of Lazarus, He called Lazarus to come forth. The rest of the dead still remained there. Also, though Jesus came to set the captives free, He left His own cousin, John the Baptist, to stay in jail until his head was cut off.

In the story of Jacob, we see that the only person who could save Jacob made every effort to get away from him. He said to Jacob, **"Let me go, for it will soon be daylight."** But Jacob said, **"I would not let you go, unless you bless me"**. Let us also look at two New Testament Scriptures, to buttress our point.

> *"And he saw them toiling in rowing; for the wind was contrary unto them: and about the fourth watch of the night he cometh unto them, walking upon the sea, and would have passed by them."* Mark 6:48

This was Jesus. He saw His disciples troubled in the sea. In spite of the fact that He knew they had problems, He set His face as if He was going to pass by, and the Bible says that He would have passed, but then they saw Him and cried out. He stopped, and they laid hold on Him.

> *"And they drew nigh unto the village, whither they went: and he made as though he would have gone further."* Luke 24:28

This was Jesus again. He was talking to His people, and when they got close to where they would stay, He kept His face as if He was going further. Is it that God wants to avoid us? No!, but through what looks as if He is going to avoid us, He ignites a fire in us, or stirs up enough action in us. For us to be like Jacob, who said, "Unless thou bless me I will not let you go," there has to be a stirring. When we are stirred up like that, then we will look for God with all our hearts. Please pray again like this: "Power to lay hold on God like Jacob, fall upon me, so that God will not pass me by, in Jesus' name."

29

WHAT IS SICKNESS?

Sickness is a state of bad health; when things that are meant to be functioning well are not. The Bible makes us to understand that there are different kinds of sicknesses, namely:

1. **Spiritual sickness:** This is the sickness of the spirit. Once the spirit is sick, it can lead to other problems in the body and in the soul. Such sicknesses are generally caused by sin. Spiritual sickness will result in spiritual weakness or lack of appetite, just like somebody who is sick physically. A person may have spiritual Kwashiorkor, meaning that his spirit is poorly fed, suffering from bad nutrition, and cannot contend against the enemy of the soul.

2. **Emotional sickness:** This sickness is caused by the hurting or damaging of the emotions. It is common with people who are easily upset.

3.   **Mind sickness:** This is when the mind, the will, and the intellect   behave abnormally. Dirty minds, weak wills, ungodly imagination, unprogressive thinking, blindness of the heart, and blankness of the heart, are signs of a sick mind. They cannot be seen physically but manifest through people's attitudes.

4.   **Sickness of the body:** This is when the body is not functioning well in one part or the other. Many people understand the sickness of the body. If you understand the sickness of the body, it is not difficult to understand what it would look like if the spirit is sick. If you have ever had malaria fever, imagine how you felt at that time, then imagine how you would feel if your spirit were to have fever. When the enemy knows that the spirit is sick, he comes in and strikes. This is the major cause of sudden death; weak spirit falling under the sledgehammer of the enemy.

5.   **Demonic sicknesses:** In these cases, nothing is wrong with the body but certain spirits are hiding there, causing trouble and confusion. These are diseases sponsored by bad spirits.

31

6.   **Sicknesses unto death:** These sicknesses are sponsored by the spirit of death and hell.

Man has always had his own way of treating sicknesses. God too, has His own method of treating sicknesses, and the devil has his own method. When you accept the devil's treatment, it is like accepting treatment from a quack doctor. There are many quack doctors who treat people the wrong way. Going to the devil for treatment, amounts to the same thing. When a person accepts the devil's treatment, many other problems will follow. It does not matter how long you have received the treatment.

DEMONIC ARROWS
and your
HEALTH

A lot of health problems are traceable to demonic arrows. These arrows lead to the following results:

1.   **Multiplication of sorrows:** The Bible says, the sorrow of those who run to other gods, shall be multiplied.
2.   **Selling yourself to the devil for nothing, as pointed out:**
     The Bible says,

     "For thus saith the Lord, ye have sold yourselves for nought and ye shall be redeemed without money." Isaiah 52:3

3. **Engaging in primitive spiritual trade by barter:** Since the devil has the power to put sickness in people, he also has the power to withdraw some of the sickness, so that the victim would be confused and will eventually be captured and thrown into hell fire.

4. **Exchange of destiny:** This happens when you go to the hospital of the enemy for treatment.

5. **The entire body of the person could be exchanged by wicked spirit:** People whose containers, called "the body", have been exchanged, are not difficult to recognise. They suffer heaviness, drowsiness, and are very vulnerable to spiritual wounds, because they are carrying a body which does not belong to them. Once you have a body that does not belong to you, you cannot get married in that state, because no husband or wife will marry a fake body. The hospital can never find out what is wrong because when you get there, the evil powers would quickly replace it with the normal body, and the doctors would not see anything wrong, but when you are out, they quickly put the bad one back. These days, they do that a lot.

The bodies of many people are under remote control. The bodies really do not belong to them, and this is the reason the bodies are opposed to their spirits. The bodies are acting in opposition to their spirits. This is why some people experience unexplainable hatred. Some people who are meant to help them, just hate them. All these happen, when you go for treatment in the hospital of the devil.

6. **Unconscious spiritual transportation:** Ten years ago, a little girl of seven was brought to me. The person, who brought her said, "Tell the man of God what you have been doing." She said, "I used to carry my mother to witchcraft meetings, although she is not a witch, but I carry her there." I asked for her mother to see me, and she was brought in. The woman was supposed to be in her 30s, but looked like a woman of 60.

During the journey to the witchcraft meetings at night, she received wounds. Her head was hit against things, even her spirit too, as she was carried all over the place. Physically, she suffered constant sicknesses including suicidal tendencies bothering on insanity, and she felt things moving about in her body. This was because one day, the woman went for treatment in the hospital of the devil, and from then, her case file was transferred to her daughter, who started to use her as a house to go for witchcraft meetings. If you are like that and you are reading this, you shall be set loose, in Jesus' name.

7.   **When you go for treatment in the camp of the enemy, you put yourself in the cooking pot of the enemy:** This is why some people complain about heat and peppery feeling all over their body. Such people are tied down, so that they keep going back to consult the evil powers until they are finished with them. Your lot will not be like that, in Jesus' name.

When a call goes out in the world of wickedness to get a person, the dark powers will first of all check their records, to see if they have anything on the person. Once the person has consulted them or has been to their saloon, he or she would be in trouble. When a person goes to a barbing salon called "Hot-head", he or she is looking for trouble because they did not mince words on their notice board. What they do there is well spelt out. So do not be surprised if the person's head is messed up. They would use the hair collected from the person for evil. The same goes for those who have kissed their agents. They will use their saliva for evil. They can also use their clothes, photographs, etc. They start working on people from these point.

THE DEMONIC BANK

If you carry your body to satanic agents, they will remove all they want and keep them in their bank. With incisions, they gain access to people's blood for future manipulation. Such people are also marked. All the stylish things people put on their stomach and hands for example tattoos, are bad marks which need to be cleaned up by the blood of Jesus. When they put incision on your body, you form the strongest covenant on earth called the blood covenant. If you have been treated with incisions before, you need to get hold of the Great Physician now. All those who say they heal through incisions, are physicians of no value.

Maybe you have been asked to carry sacrifices. All they have done is to convert you to the devil's caterer. You have fed wandering spirits at the crossroads. You have cooked food for them, and now you expect them to leave you alone. No, they will multiply your problems, so that you will bring more food. All those who have their bath with charmed soap, are busy washing away their virtues and transferring them to somebody else. Using strange perfumes on the body would result in chasing away the good spirits that would have helped you.

HERBAL TRAPS

Eating herbal concoction is the same thing as feeding from the devil's table. There is a book called, "Demons, Doctors and Medicine." It reveals the secrets of satanic agents who are doctors or nurses. According to the book, they do not treat patients, but kill them softly. They are physicians of no value. Bathing in the river, at the prescription of a herbalist or fake prophet leads to evil initiation to water spirits. They are making you a disciple of the mermaid.

When because of one problem or the other somebody has sex with a herbalist or a so-called man of God, all he or she is doing is signing off his or her own marriage, and inviting stubborn spirit husband or spirit wife. Some people would be told that before they can get out of a problem, they have to go under the bridge and have sex with a mad woman or mad man. What they are doing to them is initiation into spiritual madness.

The Bible says that when you join yourself to a harlot, you become one body. The person becomes one body with madness. Such people need deliverance. A certain woman was seeking for a child and was told by a herbalist to buy a young goat, carry it on her back, and walk to a market place. What the herbalist did was to give her a goat for a child. The child was already a child of hell fire even before he was born.

EVIL METHODS

These are the methods of the physicians of no value. They have caused people a lot of terror and havoc, especially in the black man's world. Their cures are uncertain, indefinite and unreliable, but when the cure is from the Lord Jesus Christ, it is certain. The Bible says that all that come to Him, He will in no wise cast out. He cures all that come to Him. Jesus can also cure instantly. He cures perfectly, permanently, and most importantly, He cures without charging anything.

EVIL SPIRITUAL SERVICE

If you have ever paid anybody for giving you spiritual service, know for sure that the service you paid for was not from God. He says, "Freely are you given, freely you give." When somebody charges you money because he wants to bless anointing oil, he is not from God. Somebody came to me and said that a prophet charged him N4000 for anointing oil, which should cost only N25.

The Lord Jesus Christ is the perfect doctor of both spiritual and physical diseases. If we can remove all the spiritual diseases, nobody will be sick again. As far as men are getting spiritually sick and are going to physicians of no value for treatment, trouble will continue to happen. If you study the people that Jesus healed in the Bible, you can group them into eight classes.

41

HEALING
in the SCRIPTURES

Healing is God's favourite meal for the believers. God takes delight in healing the sick. The scripture is replete with records of healing. Let us examine them:

1.   **The blind:** Those who are spiritually blind are unable to see the truth. They only possess physical eyes. Believers who have only physical eyes and cannot see into the spirit, are heading for danger. A certain sister visited the man she planned to marry. During the visit, she said, "Let us pray." As they prayed, the sister saw that she was no longer in the sitting room where they were, and the person sitting beside her had turned to a snake with three legs.

She opened her eyes several times but saw the man still praying, and not a snake. She was afraid of saying "no" right away. So after the prayer, she politely told the brother that she needed to pray some more about his proposal. Suppose her eyes were not opened, she would have married a three-legged snake-man. Believers who cannot see beyond their nose, go to the camp to pray for two weeks and come back to say that they did not receive anything. It is spiritual blindness.

Many people have spiritual cataract in their eyes. They see nothing in the spirit just like the physically blind people. Such a person could have lots of accidents. A spiritually blind person too, will have accidents. They fall into pits that they are not meant to fall into. The enemy would bring in a sword and they will not see him. A lot of people will be in perfect health if their eyes can open like that of Elisha because, immediately the enemy is bringing the evil parcel to you, you will see it and say, "Please, oga, this is not the address," but when you cannot see, what do you do?

God called a man some years ago and told him that an epidemic of disease was about to enter his town: "It will enter at exactly 2.00am. Therefore take your Bible, go and wait for it at the gate of town." The man said, "Oh Lord, what will I tell the spirit?"

The Lord said, "I will tell you when you get there. One step at a time." He took off and stayed there.

Truly, at exactly that time, the spirit came with a calabash to sprinkle its contents on everybody in the town, apart from those who had the concerning of the blood of Jesus. The man of God saw the thing and said, "Stop, in the name of Jesus." The thing said, "Why did you stop me?" He said, "Because I don't want you to go there and put your sickness on the people." The thing said, "What? But, we have our own children there, too. You people are causing trouble. You should protect only your own children, and leave us alone to punish our own." The man of God said, "No, the Bible says that God maketh the rain to fall on both the just and the unjust." He said, "No, I am not talking about rain now. I am talking about sickness." They argued for a long time. Let us open our eyes. We need them open. It is important.

44

2. **Jesus healed the deaf and the dumb:** There are people who come to the house of God but they never hear the voice of God. They have no fire in their tongue and cannot discuss with God spiritually. They need to hear the voice of the Lord today. For the string that is tying their tongues and ears to be loosed, they need to be able to hear the voice of God calling them by name. God has to call you by name, and you will answer.

3. **Jesus healed the lame:** The spiritually lame people are those who cannot walk in God's way. They find it so difficult to keep to the path of holiness. Their legs are not equal. They remain in the valley because of the difficulty of climbing to the mountain. People are looking over their heads, but they do not look at the legs. They do not even know that the legs have injury, and are lame. A lame man cannot win a 100 meters race against people with normal legs. If there is fire in a place, the lame man has to be helped, just like the blind has to be helped.

4.   **Jesus healed lepers:** These are people who are unclean by reason of their sin. Sin is the leprosy of the soul, and lepers are usually kept away from other persons. They are kept outside the town. Spiritual leprosy will keep you away from God's blessings and from getting your benefits from the Lord.

5.   **Jesus healed the crooked, the withered and the paralytic:** These are people whose spiritual lives are paralysed. They are useless in God's army. Sin has removed their strength, and sicknesses have taken over. They do not correct what they should correct, so they go to physicians of no value and they add more to their problems.

6.   **Jesus healed fever and the issue of blood:** Spiritually, this means uncontrollable passion for sin and spiritual leakage resulting in lack of discipline.

7. **Jesus healed the demon possessed:** These were people imprisoned in the body, soul and spirit, by foul spirits. Such people are a curse to themselves, and a danger to others. They need to be set free.

8. **Jesus raised the dead:** He prayed for the dead to come back to life. There are those who are dead in trespasses and sins; dead towards God. As far as God is concerned, they do not exist.

Beloved, why don't you go to Jesus today for your healing. Pay no price, for He heals for free. Go at once, because if you delay and neglect it, it may mean death. When you do not go for your treatment with the Great Physician, you can be eaten up. It does not matter how heavily you have been bombarded, there is the balm of Gilead. All you have to do today is to cry unto God. The scripture says, "Call upon me in the day of trouble and I will answer and thou shall glorify my name."

A SHOCK.

I remember the story of a man who runs a pharmacy shop and used to think that he was very bright. He had a Christian friend who used to preach to him. He would always argue and refuse to believe. One day, the Christian said, "Well, I am not going to talk to you about salvation again, but remember, any day you run into trouble I give you one verse; which says, "Call upon me in the day of trouble. I will deliver thee and thou shall glorify me," and he went away.

A few weeks later, the man was sleeping in his shop and a little girl came with a prescription from a doctor. She said her mother was sick to the point of death and needed some drugs. The pharmacist was unhappy to be woken up, yet half asleep, he gave the girl the medicine. Immediately the small girl got it, she ran out to give it to her mother. Not quite a minute after the girl left, as the pharmacist was putting the drug container back on the shelf, he discovered that instead of the correct medicine, he had poured poison into the bottle he gave to that little girl.

FORCED TO PRAY

Immediately, his sleep cleared. He ran out, looked to the left and to the right, but could not see the girl. He was distressed. He shouted, but the little girl did not come back. He was worried because he knew that when the drug is given to the woman, and she died, somebody would find out the truth and he would be in trouble.

He ran back into his room and the Scripture verse of his friend occurred to him: "Call upon me in the day of trouble and I will answer, and thou shall glorify my name". The man started praying and crying, "God, if you will only do this, I will believe that you exist and will give you my life." Immediately he finished praying, he had not risen from the floor when the little girl was at the door again.

She had fallen down and broken the bottle. She said, "Excuse me sir, I broke the bottle because I was in a hurry." The man wondered, "So this is how God works? He then committed his life to the Lord completely. Now, if God could do that for that man, He will do it for you also.

PRAYER POINTS

1. I oppose every evil influence, that the enemy is having over my life, in Jesus' name.
2. Any material of my body present in any evil altar be withdrawn, in the name of Jesus.
3. Any good thing belonging to me, that is presently being kept in a satanic bank, be released to me, in the name of Jesus.
4. Any area I have submitted myself to physicians of no value, be released in the name of Jesus.
5. I release myself from every infirmity, in the name of Jesus.
6. Eternal Rock of ages, lay your hands of fire upon me, in Jesus' name
7. Lord Jesus, answer me when I cry, in Jesus' name.

OTHER BOOKS BY DR. D. K. OLUKOYA

51

YORUBA PUBLICATIONS

1. ADURA AGBAYORI
2. ADURA TI NSI OKE NIDI ·
3. OJO ADURA

FRENCH PUBLICATIONS

1. PLUIE DE PRIÈRE
2. ESPIRIT DE VAGABONDAGE
3. EN FINIR AVEC LES FORCES MALÉFIQUES DE LA MAISON DE TON PÉRE
4. QUE l'ENVOUTEMENT PÉRISSE
5. FRAPPEZ l'ADVERSAIRE ET IL FUIRA
6. COMMENT RECEVIOR LA DÉLIVRANCE DU MARI ET DE LA FEMME DE NUIT
7. COMMENT SE DÉLIVRER SOI-MÊME
8. POUVOIR CONTRE LES TERRORITES SPIRITUELS
9. PRIÈRE DE PERCÉES POUR LES HOMMES D'AFFAIRES
10. PRIER JUSQU'À REMPORTER LA VICTOIRE
11. PRIÈRES VIOLENTES POUR HUMILIER LES PROBLÈMES OPINIÂTRES
12. PRIÈRE POUR DÉTRUIRE LES MALADIES ET LES INFIRMITÉS
13. LE COMBAT SPIRITUEL ET LE FOYER

ANNUAL 70 DAYS PRAYER AND FASTING PUBLICATIONS

1. Prayers That Bring Miracles
2. Let God Answer By Fire
3. Prayers To Mount With Wings As Eagles
4. Prayers That Bring Explosive Increase
5. Prayers For Open Heavens
6. Prayers To Make You Fulfil Your Divine Destiny
7. Prayers That Make God To Answer And Fight By Fire
8. Prayers That Bring Unchallengeable Victory And Breakthrough Rainfall Bombardments
9. Prayers That Bring Dominion Prosperity And Uncommon Success
10. Prayers That Bring Power And Overflowing Progress
11. Prayers That Bring Laughter And Enlargement Breakthroughs
12. Prayers That Bring Uncommon Favour And Breakthroughs
13. Prayers That Bring Unprecedented Greatness & Unmatchable Increase
14. Prayers That Bring Awesome Testimonies And Turn Around Breakthroughs

ABOUT THE BOOK

Healing through Prayer is a powerful presentation of the power of prayer when it comes to the area of healing and health. Using familiar Bible passages, the author has traced instances of healing from Genesis to Revelation. He maintains that God is the healer and that prayer is a means of grace for procuring one of the benefits of redemption; healing. There are easy to follow instructions and prayers for total healing. The word of God as an agent of healing is also upheld. This book contains healing tablets that will give you soundness of health and keep you healthy.

about the AUTHOR

Dr. D. K. Olukoya is the General Overseer of the Mountain of Fire and Miracles Ministries and The Battle Cry Christian Ministries.

The Mountain of Fire and Miracles Ministries' Headquarters is the largest single christian congregation in Africa with attendance of over 120,000 in single meetings.

MFM is a full gospel ministry devoted to the revival of Apostolic signs, Holy Ghost Fireworks, miracles and the unlimited demonstration of the power of God to deliver to the uttermost. Absolute holiness within and without as spiritual insecticide and pre-requisite for heaven is openly taught. MFM is a do-it-yourself Gospel Ministry, where your hands are trained to wage war and your fingers to do battle.

Dr. Olukoya holds a first class honours degree in Micro-biology from the University of Lagos and a PhD in Molecular Genetics from the University of Reading, United Kingdom. As a researcher, he has over seventy scientific publications to his credit.

Anointed by God, Dr. Olukoya is a prophet, evangelist, teacher and preacher of the Word. His life and that of his wife, Shade and their son, Elijah Toluwani are living proofs that all power belongs to God.

978-978-8424-35-2

Printed in Great Britain
by Amazon